Peace Begins With Me

A Collection of Poems

Jill Bennett

OXFORD
UNIVERSITY PRESS

OXFORD
UNIVERSITY PRESS

Great Clarendon Street, Oxford OX2 6DP

Oxford University Press is a department of the University of Oxford.
It furthers the University's objective of excellence in research, scholarship,
and education by publishing worldwide in

Oxford New York

Athens Auckland Bangkok Bogotá Buenos Aires
Cape Town Chennai Dar es Salaam Delhi Florence Hong Kong Istanbul
Karachi Kolkata Kuala Lumpur Madrid Melbourne Mexico City Mumbai
Nairobi Paris São Paulo Shanghai Singapore Taipei Tokyo Toronto Warsaw

with associated companies in Berlin Ibadan

Oxford is a registered trade mark of Oxford University Press
in the UK and in certain other countries

This selection and arrangement copyright © Jill Bennett 2001

Illustrations copyright © Peter Bailey 2001

The moral rights of the author have been asserted

First published 2001

British Library Cataloguing in Publication Data available

ISBN 0-19-276232-X

1 3 5 7 9 10 8 6 4 2

Typeset by Mary Tudge (Typesetting Services)

Printed in the UK by Cox & Wyman Ltd, Reading, Berkshire

For John Logan
Om, shanti, shanti, shanti

Contents

Walk on a Rainbow Trail

Let There Be Peace

Let there be peace on earth
And let it begin with me.
Let there be peace on earth
And let it begin in my heart.
Let there be miracles on earth
And let them begin with my faith.
Let there be a future
And let it begin with my action—now.

Author unknown

All in the Mind

Peace is a bird,
white-feathered
as a winter tree
frothed in snow.

It is silence
leaking from cupped
hands like ice-cold
mountain water.

Peace is a petal
on the summer wind,
fine-spun as a
dragonfly's wing.

It is a promise
straddling the skies
like a rainbow
after the storm.

Moira Andrew

I Hate and I Love

I Hate and I Love

I hate and I love.
And if you ask me how,
I do not know: I only feel it,
and I'm torn in two.

Catullus

Shame

There's a girl at school
we teased her today;
made jokes, called her names.
My friends all laughed,
called it harmless fun,
said it was just a game.

Now I'm at home
feeling horrid inside,
long gone that thoughtless grin.
How will I face her
tomorrow at school?
I wish I hadn't joined in.

Tracey Blance

Anger

I was horrid.
I was bad.
Nobody guessed
what thoughts I had;

Nobody heard
the words I said,
stiff and furious
in bed.

Hatred boiled
under my skin . . .
Why did I ever
let it in?

Come the morning,
it had gone.
Clean, I was,
as a salt-licked stone.

Forgiveness touched me
like a sea,
and washed the anger
out of me.

Jean Kenward

What She Did

What she did
was really awful
It made me feel quite ill
It was wrong and quite unlawful
I feel queasy still.

What she did
was quite uncalled for
How could she be so cruel?
My friends were all appalled, for
she made me look a fool.

What she did
was out of order
It made me blush and wince
From that instant I ignored her
and haven't spoken since.

What she did
was really rotten.
But what it was
I've quite forgotten.

Roger McGough

Armour

This vest
I am wearing
is so wordproof

that nothing
you say
could possibly

hurt me
not even
if you call me

all the names
under the sun
or insult

my mother
not even
if you embarrass me

or try to make
a fool of me
in public.

Ouch!

This vest
must have
a hole in it.

Norman Silver

Growing

I can grow peace.
I can grow war.
I can grow tall
as my own front door.

I can grow dark—
and you will find
I can light candles
in the mind.

I can grow gentle,
I can grow sweet
as grass and buttercups
round my feet;

Or I can slash
and stamp and shout
and drive the Bird of Kindness
   O
      U
        T

Jean Kenward

Best Friends

Sybil says:

If you don't let me ride the bike
    And push the doll's pram—

If you don't let me be the mum
    And you be all the children—

If you don't let me be the queen
    And you be all the peasants—

If you don't let me swing
    And you do all the pushing—

Then I won't like you any more and
    I won't be your friend.

So I say:

. . . OK—and let her.

Because I couldn't
    Ride and push and swing,
    Be the mummy and the queen
All on my own . . .
                    Could I?

Mick Gowar

An Old Friend

September beckons winter in, you wonder
How this new green coat
Will fare against the wind
And how this frail friend
You found in first day fear
Will stand
When battles start.

You wander in new corridors
Pursued by different faces
In a different game
Through cold uncharted places
Where different voices call your name
And one says Paki
(That's the same).

Mike Kivi

Watching

Where I am now
there is turmoil—
pushing and shouting . . . boys
out in the playground,
fighting: an
angry noise.

Someone is bruised
and crying.
Someone has tossed a stone
right through the classroom
window.
I am alone,

But in the blue-grey
distance
I can watch the swallows race
over the edge of summer,
and lift my face.

Jean Kenward

Names

They call you names for the fun of it,
To make your insides weak,
To injure all of your happiness
And tell you you're a SIKH.

To them you're totally different,
To them you're Lower Class,
They'll hit you and hurt you as much as they can
Till your insides are eaten at last.

They say that you're brown and they hate you,
And they never go away,
They've become a part of your life now,
And I fear they're here to stay.

Kiran Chahal

Lisa

Lisa's father is
Black
And her mother is
White,
And her skin is a
Cinnamon
Delight,
Her hair is
Dark
And her eyes are
Light,
And Lisa is
Lisa,
Day and
Night.

And Lisa is
Lisa,
Night and
Day,
Though there are
People
Who sometimes
Say—
Well, Lisa is
That,
Or is Lisa
This?—
Lisa is
Everything
She is.

Lisa is
Lisa,
Day and
Night,
And her skin is a
Cinnamon
Delight,
And Lisa is
Sun
And Lisa is
Star,
And Lisa is
All
The Dreams that
Are.

Beverly McLoughland

Skin

Teacher says I have many colours in my skin.
Some colours are thick. Some colours are thin.
I have a bit of everything mixed in . . .
browns, whites, blacks, pinks too
some of my veins are a greeny blue.
Teacher said it is a sad fact
that so many people only ever see black.

Pauline Stewart

Rainbow

Yesterday
my grandma said,
'There's all the colours of the rainbow
in your school.'

I knew that she was wrong.

We have no orange people,

nor green nor blue,

and you couldn't say
That Tony Wong was yellow,

more a pale and liquid gold
like corn ripening
under autumn sun.

You could say Ingrid
is close to white
with skin you can nearly see through;

Merle's is sleek and polished black,
lovely as a glossy plum,

but nobody is indigo or violet.

I am the only one
that turns red on a sunny day,

but mostly I am pinky grey
and so that doesn't count.

Today we went outside
measuring the playground.

'Give me your hand,' said Rashid.
Ahmed held his,
then Marita, Marvin, May Ling,
Yana, Zamato, Peter, and the rest.

We found our playground is
exactly thirty children wide

and now we're working out
how many it would take
to go right round the earth.

We painted our own pictures
and our teacher put them on the wall.

Underneath she wrote:
Friendship between children is like a rainbow.
It stretches right across the world.

So after all my gran was right.

Barrie Wade

All of Us

All of us are afraid
More often than we tell.

There are times we cling like mussels to the sea-wall,
And pray that the pounding waves
Won't smash our shell.

Times we hear nothing but the sound
Of our loneliness, like a cracked bell
From fields far away where the trees are in icy shade.

O many a time in the night-time and in the day,
More often than we say,
We are afraid.

If people say they are never frightened,
I don't believe them.
If people say they are frightened,
I want to retrieve them
From that dark shivering haunt
Where they don't want to be,
Nor I.

Let's make ourselves, therefore, an enormous sky
Over whatever
We most hold dear.

And we'll comfort each other,
Comfort each other's
Fear.

Kit Wright

A Trade

I'll trade you my kingdom for your song
I'll trade you my song for your colour
I'll trade you my colour for your story
I'll trade you my story for your dance
I'll trade you my dance for your daydream
I'll trade you my daydream for your hand
I'll trade you my hand for your hand

Zaro Weil

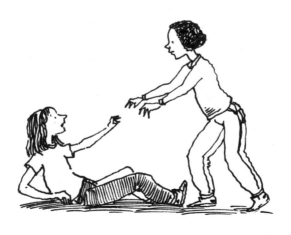

The Runners

We're hopeless at racing,
Me and my friend.
I'm slow at the start,
She's slow at the end.

She has the stitch,
I get sore feet,
And neither of us
Cares to compete.

But co-operation's
A different case.
You should see us
In the three-legged race!

Allan Ahlberg

Tell Me Why

Tell Me Why?

Daddy will you tell me why
There are no battleships in the sky?
    The reason is apparently
    They only battle on the sea

Then will you tell me if you please
Why grandfather clocks cannot sneeze?
    The reason is, or so I'm told
    They're too stupid and too old

Will you explain once and for all
Why Little Jack Horner fell off the wall?
    It wasn't him it was Little Bo Peep
    Now be a good boy and go to sleep

Daddy will you tell me when
Little boys grow into men?
    Some never do that's why they fight
    Now kiss me, let me hold you tight

For in the morning I must go
To join my regiment and so
    For Queen and country bravely die
    Son, oh son, please tell me why?

Roger McGough

My Dad

My dad says:

after the war was over
everyone came home
to sort things out

there weren't going to be any more wars
there weren't going to be any more poor people
there weren't going to be any more bad houses
there weren't going to be any more people out of work

that was forty years ago

now they're trying to invent space ships
that drop bombs.

Michael Rosen

War

Here is the quarrel
you wouldn't end;
Here is the hate
that wounds a friend;
Here is anger,
here is spite,
here are the bullets
that flew all night;
Here are sharp words,
here are knives;
Here, the remains
of shattered lives.

Lois Rock

War

A group of eight year olds
follow me into a room.
Three boys, three girls.
'Let's move the table,' I say.
We all move the table.
'Who's going behind the table?' I say.
'Me,' says one of the boys—
'Get away from the girls,' he says.
After eight years alive in this world
we have taught him to be at war
with half the people in the world.

Michael Rosen

Uncle Harry

Uncle Harry, back from war
Uncle Harry, knocks the door
Uncle Harry, currant bun
Uncle Harry, bags of fun
       Happy Harry, full of play
       Family comic, grown-ups say
       Magic fingers
       Tricks galore
       Jolly Harry at the door . . .
Uncle Harry, let him in
       Likes to giggle, likes to grin
Clever Harry, family card
       Handsome lad and parlour bard . . .
Joking Harry—what a star
       Uncle Harry—he'll go far!
       Family favourite
       Brother—Son
         —Uncle Harry
           Here he comes!
So, wave your flag
Fling wide that door . . .

Uncle Harry, back from war

Peter Dixon

Does it Matter?

Does it matter?—losing your legs? . . .
For people will always be kind,
And you need not show that you mind
When the others come in after hunting
To gobble their muffins and eggs.

Does it matter?—losing your sight? . . .
There's such splendid work for the blind;
And people will always be kind,
As you sit on the terrace remembering
And turning your face to the light.

Do they matter?—those dreams from the pit? . . .
You can drink and forget and be glad,
And people won't say that you're mad;
For they'll know you've fought for your country
And no one will worry a bit.

Siegfried Sassoon

Holocaust

'First they came for the Jews
and I did not speak out—
because I was not a Jew

Then they came for the communists
and I did not speak out—
because I was not a communist

Next they came for the trade unionists
and I did not speak out—
because I was not a trade unionist

Then they came for me
and there was no one left
to speak out for me.'

Pastor Niemoeller

The Butterfly

The last, the very last,
So richly, brightly, dazzlingly yellow.
Perhaps if the sun's tears would sing
  against a white stone . . .

Such, such a yellow
Is carried lightly 'way up high.
It went away I'm sure because it wished to
  kiss the world goodbye.

For seven weeks I've lived in here,
Penned up inside this ghetto.
But I have found what I love here.
The dandelions call to me
And the white chestnut branches in the court.
Only I never saw another butterfly.

That butterfly was the last one.
Butterflies don't live in here,
  in the ghetto.

Pavel Friedmann

Poppies in the Park

There were poppies in the park today
with stems of sanded pine
and names like Dick
      and Dad
      and Dave
with words like Passchendaele.
Words like Somme
      Dunkirk
      and Loos
and some more foreign too
some Chinese names like Long Tung Sung
and ones like Sung Hong Soo.
There were crosses in the park today,
all splashed with football mud
with—
THANK YOU UNCLE ARNOLD
and
THANK YOU CORPORAL RUDD.
So 'thank you' Sergeant Fellows
and 'thank you' Enid's dad
for dying for your country—
I wish I could feel sad.

Peter Dixon

In Memoriam (Easter, 1915)

The flowers left thick at nightfall in the wood
This Eastertide call into mind the men,
Now far from home, who, with their sweethearts, should
Have gathered them and will never do again.

Edward Thomas

The Cherry Trees

The cherry trees bend over and are shedding,
On the old road where all that passed are dead,
Their petals, strewing the grass as for a wedding
This early May morn when there is none to wed.

Edward Thomas

Peace in Our Time

PEACE!
PEACE IN OUR TIME scream
the yellowing headlines.
A fuzzy photograph, an
old man in a Homburg hat
waves a piece of paper.

PEACE!
'Give me a bit of peace,'
yells our mother. We rattle
up and downstairs paying
not the slightest bit of
attention. Mother sighs.

PEACE!
The bells ring out. A new
era is ushered in. Children
of the war, knowing only
blackout and rations learn
the new taste of bananas.

PEACE!
'Grant me peace,' whispers
our mother as she lies dying.
Pain maps its contour lines
across her face. Her peace
is forever, ours touch and go.

Moira Andrew

Just Another War

On her sideboard
Nan has a picture
Of a young man
In a soldier's uniform
Smiling proudly.

'That's my brother,
Your Uncle Reg.'
She says,
Her voice tinged
With sadness.

'He was killed
In Korea.
He was only nineteen.'

'Where's Korea?' I say.
'What were they fighting for?'

'Somewhere in Asia,'
She says.
'I don't know.
It was just another war.'

John Foster

Kurdish Child

He longs for life without cold.
He longs for life without fear,
when the young and the frail and the old
won't ask if danger's near.

He needs to ripen and grow
as naturally as grass
where there is no ache in the heart
when a stranger's footsteps pass.

He deserves a place in the sun,
and singing birds in the sky
with never a bomb or a gun
to terrify.

And surely, we have to show
what it is we all of us share:
laughing, he needs to know
that love is there.

Jean Kenward

Another Child Has Gone Missing

A rose grows out of her head,
yellowing grass roots in her heart.
Sun shines in the eyes of the children,
dirty children on broken streets.

Somebody's child, somebody's love
has gone missing. No one looks.
Water drips from the branches of trees
when it bothers to rain.

No one looks for grains of dust
blown on a scorching mountain wind.
Tend to the needs of your children,
wash the soil from their bleeding feet.

Robin Mellor

The Child On Our Telly

There's a child on our telly
He's about the same age as me
Lives a million miles away
In a place I'll never see

There's a child on our telly
Who looks a bit like me
Except she is tired and hungry
While I sit here and eat my tea

There's a child on our telly
Whose life just doesn't seem real
I wish he could share what I have
And feel the way I feel

There's a child on our telly
It just doesn't seem fair
When I have and waste so much
Then say I've none to spare

There's a child on our telly
You're so full of pain and sorrow
Dad wants to watch something else
I'll think of you again tomorrow

Hugh Williams

Stop the War

Stop the war and the fighting
for a smile on a child's face.
Stop the planes and the shells
for a smile on a child's face.

Stop all the army vehicles
for a smile on a child's face.
Stop everything that kills and destroys
for a smile of happiness on a child's face.

Ivana (aged 11, from Cepin)

War is the Saddest Word

War is the saddest word that flows from my quivering lips.
It is a wicked bird that never comes to rest. It is a deadly
bird that destroys our homes, and deprives us of our
childhood. War is the evilest of birds, turning the streets red
with blood, and the world into an inferno.

Maida (aged 12, from Skopje)

From a Distance

From a distance
The world looks blue and green
And the snow-capped mountains white

From a distance
The ocean meets the sea
And the eagle takes to flight

From a distance there is harmony
And it echoes through the land
It's the voice of hope
It's the voice of peace
It's the voice of every man

From a distance
We all have enough
And no one is in need
There are no guns, no bombs, no diseases
No hungry mouths to feed

From a distance we are instruments
Marching in a common band
Playing songs of hope
Playing songs of peace
They're the songs of every man

God is watching us, God is watching us
God is watching us from a distance

From a distance
You look like my friend
Even though we are at war
From a distance I can't comprehend
What all this war is for

From a distance there is harmony
And it echoes through the land
It's the hope of hopes
It's the love of loves
It's the heart of every man

It's the hope of hopes
It's the love of loves
It's the song of every man

Julie Gold

Refugee

He can't speak a word of English
But the picture he paints needs no words

In it he puts:

guns
bright orange explosions
a house with no roof
children with no shoes
and his mother and father
lying still, as though asleep.
At the bottom he puts himself, tiny and dark,
with a puddle of blue tears at his feet.
Somehow the fat yellow sun at the top of the page
has a smile on its face.

Lindsay MacRae

The Wall That Walked

There once was a wall that walked—
Why not?
It got tired of standing in the same fixed spot,
So it walked.

There once was a wall that walked,
Or flowed,
Like a rover of stone across the main road.
A policeman tried to arrest it,
But it made for his boots, so he left it alone
To walk.

There once was a wall that walked
Right through
Spain, France, Belgium, and Italy too.
It rested in Germany, but people with picks
Came in the darkness and bashed at its bricks,
So it walked.

There once was a wall that walked
To China,
A nice quiet place, it couldn't think of one finer,
So it settled itself. And it's settled there still,
Draped like a rope over valley and hill,
Stretched like a wire, like a fast-asleep snake,
But some day soon now, the wall will awake,
And walk.

Richard Edwards

Song of the Refugee Child

I may be little but let me sing,
I may be a child but let me in.
What does it matter if I read or write?
You'll send me to war to learn to fight?

I am the refugee child.

I am the hungry of a hundred lands,
mine is the blood that stains the white sands,
but I'll climb your barbed wire and walls of stone
and find a free place to make a new home.

I am the refugee child.

I am the dispossessed, wandering one,
you can't kill me with your bomb and your gun.
I am the face that looks out from the night
towards your rich window with its warmth and light.

I am the refugee child.

I am a child of the family called Poor
and I am coming to knock on your door.
I may be little but let me sing,
I may be a child but you must let me in.

I am the refugee child.

Robin Mellor

Walk on a Rainbow Trail

Good Hope

I believe
There is enough food
On this planet
For everyone.

I believe
That it is possible
For all people
To live in peace.

I believe
We can live
Without guns,
I believe everyone
Is important.

I believe there are good Christians
And good Muslims,
Good Jews
And good not sures,
I believe
There is good in everyone
I believe in people.

If I did not believe
I would stop writing.

I know
Every day
Children cry for water,
And every day
Racists attack,
Still every day
Children play
With no care for colour.

So I believe **there is hope**
And I hope
That there are many believers
Believing
There is hope,
That is what I hope
And this is what I believe,
I believe in you,
Believe me.

Benjamin Zephaniah

Sea-Rock

Sea rock us to love
        rock us to love

Breeze glad us to touch
        glad us to touch

Sun shift us in strides
        shift us in strides

Trees keep the gold and green of memory
        keep the gold and green of memory

But most of all sea
        rock us to love
        rock us to love

Grace Nichols

Benediction

Thanks to the ear
that someone may hear

Thanks to the seeing
that someone may see

Thanks to feeling
that someone may feel

Thanks to the touch
that one may be touched

thanks to the flowering of white moon
and spreading shawl of black night
holding villages together

James Berry

The Birds

Here comes the cockerel:
'Cock-a-doodle-doo!
I can have a morning hymn
quite as well as you!'

Here comes the raven:
'Caw caw caw . . .
I've said it once, I've said it twice,
I've told you so before!'

Here comes the lark, with
a twitter and a trill:
'I'm going up, I'm going up,
I'm going higher still!'

Here comes the barn owl:
'Wit! To-wit-a-woo!
Silly people go to war—
what a thing to do!'

Here comes the blackbird
with his special song—
'Come and listen! Come and listen!'
All the summer long.

And here comes the dove
with an olive in her bill:
'I carry PEACE to all the world—
help me, if you will.'

Jean Kenward

Dove

The white dove
stands
for peace.

For love
Of other lands.
Your enemy.
Your friend.
Your neighbour.

Join hands.
Labour
for love.
Send
the peaceful message
of the dove.

Ann Bonner

Co-operation

Justice is a great big pot
and we are its ladle.

Can Yucel

Cathedral

Come into this quiet place where
Angels carved in stone look down on
Tombs of noble lords and ladies.
Here are stained-glass windows to delight the
Eye and tell us tales of long ago—here the Great West
Door and there an eagle spreads its wings. Here are
Rows and rows of seats and high above each aisle
Arches soar. Come into this quiet place.
Listen to its peace.

June Crebbin

Do All the Good

Do all the good you can
By all the means you can
In all the ways you can
In all the places you can
To all the people you can
As long as ever you can.

John Wesley

Kwan Yin

Kwan Yin came quietly,
settling herself on a rock by the hard sea shore.

Kwan Yin came softly,
and the waves seemed to flow like the folds of the garment
    she wore.

Down by the waters
she sat with a merciful heart that was brimming with care.

Kwan Yin's compassion
came rippling out to all creatures on radiant air:

Over the ocean,
the fish and the heron, the squid, the insomniac shark,

Over the daylight,
beyond the horizon, to soften the gathering dark,

Over the land,
where the ox and the farmer went ploughing with regular
    feet,

Over the cities,
where princes and beggars were born to their high and
    low station,

Over the world,
with its curious customs and cultures, from nation to nation,

Up to the heavens,
where planets and comets and stars shone like silver above,

Kwan Yin sat quietly,
steadily giving her care and compassionate love.

Tony Mitton

Peace is Every Step

Peace is every step.
The shining red sun is my heart.
Each flower smiles with me.
How green, how fresh all that grows.
How cool the wind blows.
Peace is every step.
It turns the endless path to joy.

Thich Nhat Hanh

The Messenger

Can there be life beyond the stars,
far out of sight,
where people have no battle scars—
nor wish to fight?

Or could there be another place
shining, and good,
where lurk no secret enemies
in a dark wood?

Shall we receive a messenger
who will display
such wisdom to us all, perhaps
there'll come a day

When we'll put down our guns, and learn
at last to see
peace between man and beast, as it
was meant to be?

Jean Kenward

Before Me Peaceful

Before me peaceful
Behind me peaceful
Under me peaceful
Over me peaceful
Around me peaceful

Navajo prayer

Peace be to Earth

Peace be to earth and to airy space.
Peace be to heaven, peace to the waters,
Peace to the plant and peace to the trees.
May all the powers grant to me peace.

May everything for us be peaceful.

Athara Veda XIX

Perfect

That is perfect. This is perfect.
Perfect comes from perfect.
Take perfect from perfect, the remainder is perfect.
May peace and peace and peace be everywhere.

The Upanishads

May the Waters

May the waters flow peacefully,
May the herbs and plants grow peacefully,
May all the divine powers bring us peace.
The supreme lord is peace.
May we all be in peace, peace and only peace,
And may that peace come to each of us.

Shanti Shanti Shanti

from The Vedas

Deep Peace

Deep peace of the Running Wave to you
Deep peace of the Flowing Air to you
Deep peace of the Quiet Earth to you
Deep peace of the Shining Stars to you
Deep peace of the Gentle Night to you
Deep peace of the Son of Peace to you
Moon and stars pour their healing light on you
Deep peace to you.

Celtic Blessing

Walk on a Rainbow Trail

Walk on a rainbow trail;
Walk on a trail of song,
and all about you shall be beauty.

There is a way out of every dark mist,
over a rainbow trail.

Navajo song

Index of Titles and First Lines
(First lines are in Italic)

Index of Authors

Acknowledgements

We are grateful for permission to reprint copyright poems:

Anonymous poem 'Let there be Peace' from *Renewing the Earth, Study Guide for Groups*, 1989 (CAFOD), reprinted by permission of CAFOD. **Allan Ahlberg**: 'The Runners' from *Please Mrs Butler* (Kestrel, 1983), copyright © Allan Ahlberg 1983, reprinted by permission of Penguin Books Ltd. **Moira Andrew**: 'All in the Mind' and 'Peace in Our Time', copyright © Moira Andrew 1992, first published in *Dove on the Roof* edited by Jennifer Curry (Mammoth, 1992), reprinted by permission of the author. **James Berry**: 'Benediction' from *Chain of Days* (OUP, 1985), copyright © James Berry 1985, reprinted by permission of PFD on behalf of James Berry. **Tracey Blance**: 'Shame', copyright © Tracey Blance 1999, first published in *I Wanna be Your Mate* edited by Tony Bradman (Bloomsbury, 1999), reprinted by permission of the author. **Ann Bonner**: 'Dove', copyright © Ann Bonner 2001, first published in this collection by permission of the author. **Catullus**: 'I Hate and I Love' from *The Poems of Catullus* translated by Peter Whigham (Penguin Classics, 1966), translation copyright © Penguin Books 1966, reprinted by permission of Penguin Books Ltd. **Kiran Chahal**: 'Names', copyright © Kiran Chahal 1985, first published in Hillingdon NAPE Journal, Spring 1985, reprinted by permission of the author. **June Crebbin**: 'Cathedral' from *Cows Moo, Cars Toot* (Viking, 1995), copyright © June Crebbin 1995, reprinted by permission of Penguin Books Ltd. **Peter Dixon**: 'Poppies in the Park' from *Grow Your Own Poems* (Peche Luna, 1996), copyright © Peter Dixon 1988, and 'Uncle Harry' from *Penguin in the Fridge* (Macmillan, 2001), copyright © Peter Dixon 2001, both reprinted by permission of the author. **Richard Edwards**: 'The Wall that Walked' from *Leopards on Mars* (Viking, 1993), copyright © Richard Edwards 1993, reprinted by permission of the author. **John Foster**: 'Just Another War' from *Four O'Clock Friday* (OUP, 1991), copyright © John Foster 1991, reprinted by permission of the author. **Pavel Friedman**: 'The Butterfly' from *I Never Saw Another Butterfly* (Schocken Books) edited by Hana Volavkova, US Holocaust Memorial Museum, copyright © 1978, 1993 by Artia Prague, compilation copyright © 1993 by Schocken Books, forward copyright © 1993 by Chaim Potok, reprinted by permission of Schocken Books, a division of Random House, Inc. **Julie Gold**: 'From a Distance', words and music copyright © 1986 Julie Gold Music (BMI) and Wing and Wheel Music (BMI), words and music copyright © 1990 Irving Music Inc/Wing & Wheel Music/Julie Gold Music/Rondor Music (London) Ltd W6 8JA. Julie Gold Music administered worldwide by Cherry River Music Co. Wing and Wheel Music administered by Irving Music, Inc. Lyrics reproduced by permission of IMP Ltd and the Hal Leonard Corporation. International copyright secured. All rights reserved. **Mick Gowar**: 'Best of Friends' from *Third Time Lucky* (Viking Kestrel, 1988), copyright © Mick Gowar 1988, reprinted by permission of Penguin Books Ltd and David Higham Associates. **Thich Nhat Hanh**: 'Peace is Every Step' extract from *The Long Road Turns to Joy: A Guide to Walking Meditation* (1996), reprinted by permission of the publishers, Parallax Press, Berkeley, California. **Ivana**: 'Stop the War' from *I Dream of Peace: Images of War by children of former Yugoslavia* (UNESCO/HarperCollins, 1994), copyright © 1994 UNICEF, reprinted by permission of HarperCollins Publishers, Inc. **Jean Kenward**: 'Kurdish Child', copyright © Jean Kenward 1992, first published in *Can You Hear Me* (OXFAM/Macmillan 1992); 'Anger', 'Growing', 'Watching', 'The Birds' and 'The Messenger', all copyright © Jean Kenward 2001, first published in this collection; all by permission of the author. **Mike Kivi**: 'An Old Friend' from *Call the Teacher Lazy!* (Educational Printing Services, 2000), copyright © Mike Kivi 2000, reprinted by permission of the author. **Roger McGough**: 'Tell Me Why?' from *Sky in the Pie* (Viking Kestrel, 1983), copyright © Roger McGough 1983; and 'What She Did' from *Big Bad Cats* (Viking Kestrel, 1997), copyright © Roger McGough 1997, reprinted by permission of PFD on behalf of Roger McGough. **Beverly McLoughland**: 'Lisa', copyright © Beverly McLoughland 1992, first published in *Through Our Eyes: Poems and Pictures about Growing Up* chosen by Lee Bennett Hopkins (Little, Brown and Company, 1992), reprinted by permission of the author. **Lindsay MacRae**: 'Refugee' from *You Canna Shove Your Granny Off a Bus* (Viking, 1995), copyright © Lindsay MacRae 1995, reprinted by permission of Penguin Books Ltd and The Agency (London) Ltd. All rights reserved and enquiries to The Agency (London) Ltd, 24 Pottery Lane, London W11 4LZ. **Maida**: 'War is the Saddest Word' from *I Dream of Peace: Images of War by children of former Yugoslavia* (UNESCO/HarperCollins, 1994), copyright © 1994 UNICEF, reprinted by permission of HarperCollins Publishers, Inc. **Robin Mellor**: 'Another Child', copyright © Robin Mellor 2001, first published in this collection, and 'Song of the Refugee Child' first published in *Assemblies* (Scholastic, 1994), both by permission of the author. **Tony Mitton**: 'Kwan Yin', copyright © Tony Mitton 2001, first published in this collection by permission of the author. **Grace Nichols**: 'Sea-Rock' from *Give Yourself a Hug* (A & C Black, 1994), copyright © Grace Nichols 1994, reprinted by permission of Curtis Brown Ltd, London, on behalf of Grace Nichols. **Lois Rock**: 'War', copyright © Lois Rock 1997 from *Glimpses of Heaven* (Lion Publishing, 1997), reprinted by permission of the publishers. **Michael Rosen**: Lines from 'War' from *When Did You Last Wash Your Feet?* (Deutsch, 1986), copyright © Michael Rosen 1986, reprinted by permission of PFD on behalf of Michael Rosen; and 'My Dad' from *The Hypnotiser and other Skyfoogling Poems* (Deutsch, 1988), copyright © Michael Rosen 1988, reprinted by permission of the publishers, Scholastic Ltd. **Siegfried Sassoon**: 'Does It Matter?' from *Collected Poems of Siegfried Sassoon*, copyright 1918, 1920 by E P Dutton, copyright 1936, 1946, 1947, 1948 by Siegfried Sassoon, reprinted by permission of Barbara Levy Literary Agency and Viking Penguin, a division of Penguin Putnam Inc. **Norman Silver**: 'Armour' from *The Walkmen Have Landed* (Faber & Faber, 1994), copyright © Norman Silver 1994, reprinted by permission of the Laura Cecil Literary Agency on behalf of the author. **Pauline Stewart**: 'Skin' from *Singing Down the Breadfruit* (Bodley Head 1993), copyright © Pauline Stewart 1993, reprinted by permission of The Random House Group Ltd. **Barrie Wade**: 'Rainbow' from *Rainbow* (OUP), copyright © Barrie Wade 1995, reprinted by permission of the author. **Zaro Weil**: 'A Trade' from *Mud, Moon and Me* (Orchard Books, 1989), copyright © Zaro Weil 1989, reprinted by permission of the author. **Hugh Williams**: 'The Child on Our Telly', copyright © Hugh Williams 2001, first published in this collection by permission of the author. **Kit Wright**: 'All of Us' from *Great Snakes* (Viking, 1994), copyright © Kit Wright 1994, reprinted by permission of Penguin Books Ltd. **Benjamin Zephaniah**: 'Good Hope' from *Funky Chickens* (Viking, 1996), copyright © Benjamin Zephaniah 1996, reprinted by permission of Penguin Books Ltd.

Despite every effort to try to trace and contact copyright holders before publication this has not been possible in every case. If notified the publisher will be pleased to rectify any errors or omissions at the earliest opportunity.